Biomes

Deserts

Duncan Brewer

Chrysalis Children's Books

BIOMES

DESERTS
GRASSLANDS
OCEANS
RAINFORESTS
WETLANDS

Produced by Monkey Puzzle Media Ltd
Gissing's Farm, Fressingfield, Suffolk IP21 5SH, UK

First published in the UK in 2003 by
Chrysalis Children's Books
64 Brewery Road, London N7 9NT

A Belitha Book

Editor: John Woodward
Editorial Manager: Joyce Bentley
Designer: Vicky Short
Consultant: Michael Allaby
Picture Researcher: Glass Onion Pictures

ISBN: 1 84138 873 4

British Library Cataloguing in Publication Data for this book is available from the British Library.

Printed in Hong Kong/China
10 9 8 7 6 5 4 3 2 1

Picture Acknowledgements
We wish to thank the following individuals and organizations for their help and assistance, and for supplying material in their collections: Ecoscene 7 (Andrew Brown), 14 (Andrew Brown), 16 (Wayne Lawler), 23 (Sally Morgan), 31 (NASA), 38 (Karl Ammann); FLPA *front cover* (David Hosking), 1 (Chris Mattison), 3 (David Hosking), 11 (Silvestris Fotoservice), 12 (A R Hamblin), 15 (W Wisniewski), 17 (Chris Mattison), 18 (David Hosking), 19 (David Hosking), 36 (François Merlet); Robert Harding 5 top (Walter Rawlings); Panos 4 (Fred Hoogervorst), 5 bottom (Jean-Léo Dugast), 10 (Jean-Léo Dugast), 13 (Alain Le Garsmeur), 26 (Giacomo Pirozzi), 29 (Fred Hoogervorst), 33 (Jeremy Hartley), 35 (Penny Tweedie), 39 (Fred Hoogervorst), 40, 41 (Sean Sprague), 42 (Neil Cooper), 44 (Nancy Durrell McKenna), 46 (Giacomo Pirozzi), 47 (Giacomo Pirozzi); Popperfoto 27, 28 (Reuters); South American Pictures 24 (Chris Sharp), 25 (Tony Morrison); Still Pictures 5 middle (Stephen Pern), 6 (S Asad), 9 (Gordon Wiltsie), 20 (Roger De La Harpe), 21 (Ton Koene), 22 (Adrian Arbib), 30 (Gil Moti), 32 (D Escartin), 34 (Chris Caldicott), 37 (Roland Seitre), 43 (Voltchev/UNEP), 45 (John Isaac). Artwork by Michael Posen. The pictures used in this book do not show the actual people named in the case studies in the text.

CONTENTS

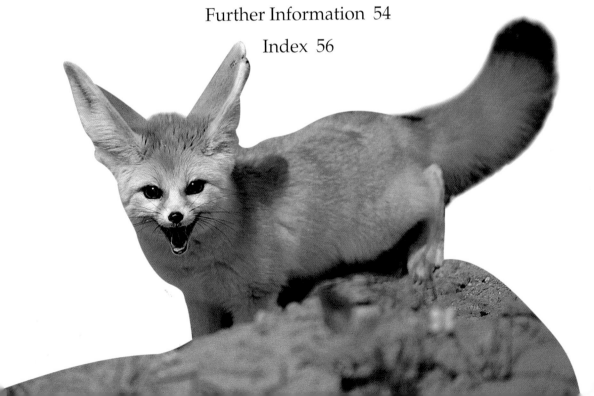

Amadou's Story

Amadou is a farmer in Niger, one of the world's poorest countries, in the dry Sahel region south of the Sahara. A succession of severe droughts in the 1970s and 1980s began to turn the land to desert, forcing Amadou off his farm. But increased rainfall has made things better, and Amadou has returned to his fields determined to grow successful crops.

'**M**Y FATHER AND my grandfather used to tell me how good village life used to be, with full granaries of millet and other crops, but when I was old enough to start taking over the family fields, those days seemed to be over. In some years the rains hardly fell at all. Hot winds from the great desert in the north shrivelled the plants and carried away the best soil.

We tried to find fertile land by clearing away trees and bushes from the region between our fields and the desert, but the crops failed because of the lack of rain, and the winds blew even stronger through the gaps we had made. The desert seemed to be growing, and it seemed ready to swallow us up.

In the end my father and I moved to the town to find work. We were able to send small amounts of money home to the family, but it was never enough. Back in the village my younger brothers tried to hunt for meat, but only ever caught a few small birds.

Then we started to get good rainy seasons again. Farmers who had stayed behind learned new ways of trapping the water and stopping the rain washing away the soil. They planted trees to hold back the desert. Eventually farmers who had moved to the town for work began to return to the villages, and my father and I moved with them. But we worry about the future. If the rains fail again, we may have to move away from our village for ever, and let the soil turn to dust.'

Who is vulnerable to desertification?

A quarter of all the people on Earth live in low-rainfall, dry regions which are under threat of being turned into deserts when droughts strike.

PATAGONIA
On the arid and treeless steppes of Argentina, over-grazing by sheep and cattle has contributed to the erosion of a large proportion of grassland pastures.

MONGOLIA
As populations have increased in the Gobi region of Mongolia, the felling of many trees for firewood has contributed to the desertification of an arid region that is already suffering from overgrazing by herds of cattle and sheep.

WEST ASIA
Traditional rangelands, grazed and farmed successfully for centuries in Jordan, Iraq and Syria, have been degraded into desert by overgrazing and the introduction of intensive farming of cereals.

What Is A Desert?

If they were asked to describe a desert, most people would use words such as sandy, flat, hot and lifeless. Yet deserts are not necessarily sandy, are often hilly, sometimes cold, and hardly ever completely without life.

TO A SCIENTIST, a desert is a region that loses more water into the air as water vapour than it receives as precipitation (rain, snow, sleet, hail, dew or frost). Deserts lose water as vapour in two ways. When water is heated by the sun it begins to evaporate, or turn to vapour. Plants also soak up water at their roots and breathe it out as vapour, in a process called transpiration.

Arid deserts receive less than 25 cm of precipitation each year. There is hardly any cloud above them during the day, and the sun heats the desert surface very quickly. The dry desert air cannot hold onto this heat at night, which is why desert nights can be bitterly cold.

What is a biome?

A biome is a major regional community of plants and animals, with similar life forms and environmental conditions. Each biome is named after its dominant feature, such as tropical rainforest, grassland, or coral reef.

Hot and cold

The highest desert air temperature ever recorded was 58°C, in Libya. 57°C has been recorded in Algeria and also in Death Valley, USA. The coldest non–polar desert temperatures are about -20°C, recorded in both the Gobi Desert and in Arizona.

Carved into a multitude of changing shapes and surface patterns by the wind, the sands of the desert often seem hostile to life at first sight.

Spanning the western border of Mexico and the USA, the Sonoran Desert is home to over 140 different species of cactus, as well as many other desert–adapted plants and animals.

Very cold regions of the Arctic and the Antarctic are called polar deserts. They are extremely dry throughout the year because all their water is locked up in ice.

There are often semi-arid regions fringing the arid deserts, where precipitation ranges between 24 cm and 90 cm each year. These are the areas where unsuitable farming methods and native plant destruction are most likely to turn the land to desert.

What are the different types of desert?

All deserts are arid, but they are arid for different reasons. There are four main processes that create deserts and keep them that way, and so there are four types of desert. They are horse-latitude deserts, continental deserts, rain-shadow deserts and coastal deserts.

The world's largest deserts, including the Sahara and the Australian deserts, lie roughly 30°N or 30°S of the Equator, in the so-called horse latitudes. Air heated up at the Equator rises, loses its moisture, and descends over these latitudes, becoming hot winds which dry up any moisture.

Continental deserts, such as the Gobi Desert of Mongolia and China, lie in the centre of the big landmasses we call continents, far from the oceans which are the source of all rainfall.

Rain-shadow deserts form near mountain ranges that cut them off from the sea. Moisture-laden air currents moving inland from oceans cool down when they rise up the slopes of these mountain barriers, and release all their moisture as rain. The dry air warms up as it flows down the opposite side of the mountains. It evaporates any local moisture, forming deserts such as America's Mojave Desert, east of the Sierra Nevada mountains.

Coastal deserts form near oceans with cool ocean currents. The air above these currents is also cool, and loses its moisture as rain at sea. The cool, dry air moves inland and creates deserts such as the Namib Desert of southwest Africa alongside the cool Benguela Current, and the Atacama Desert of south Peru and northern Chile, caused by the cool Humboldt Current.

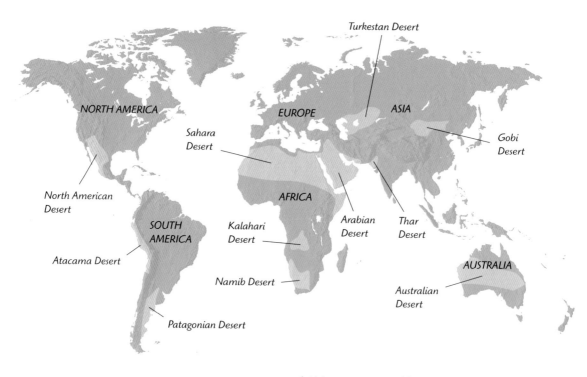

Turkestan Desert

NORTH AMERICA

EUROPE

ASIA

Sahara
Desert

Gobi
Desert

North American
Desert

AFRICA

SOUTH
AMERICA

Kalahari
Desert

Arabian
Desert

Thar
Desert

Atacama Desert

AUSTRALIA

Namib Desert

Australian
Desert

Patagonian Desert

Arid deserts

Arid deserts cover some 15 per cent of the planet's land surface, and most of them occur within broad bands centred around 30 degrees north and south of the Equator: the driest latitudes on Earth.

Where are the world's main deserts?

The Sahara is by far the world's largest desert, and one of the hottest. It stretches across 14 North African countries, with a total area of well over 9 million sq. km. There are huge areas of sand, but over two-thirds of the Sahara consists of features such as gravel plains, and mountains tall enough to have winter snows.

The Gobi Desert of Mongolia and northern China is a region of high, waterless steppes and stone-littered plains, which suffers blistering summer heat and frozen winters.

The North American Desert is a combination of four major desert areas. It ranges from the valleys and dunes of the semi-desert Great Basin, through the mountains and dried lakes of the Mojave Desert, and the cactus-studded plains of the Sonoran Desert; finally it reaches the shrubby desert lands of the Chihuahua Desert in Mexico.

The Arabian Desert is the sandiest of the great deserts. At its heart is the pure sand desert known as the Empty Quarter. This grim, inhospitable area, usually entered only by local Bedouin people, contains huge, ancient dunes.

The Kalahari Desert is at the heart of southern Africa. It varies between red sand dunes and semi-arid grasslands, and contains the Okavango Delta, Africa's largest oasis – the remains of a huge prehistoric lake.

The **Namib Desert** is a 2000-km long coastal desert: a mix of shifting dunes, rock and gravel plains. Sea fogs provide scarce moisture for plants and animals, and rainfall is no more than 25 mm per year.

The **Australian Desert** covers a large part of the continent's 'outback'. Some 70 per cent of Australia receives less than 500 mm of rain per year, and 18 per cent of the country is true desert. There are four major deserts in the western part of the continent: the Great Sandy Desert, the Gibson Desert, the Great Victoria Desert and the Simpson Desert.

The **Atacama Desert** on the western side of the Andes in South America is another coastal desert. It is the world's driest desert apart from Antarctica.

The **Patagonian Desert** is a high-altitude, cold-winter rain-shadow desert. It extends from the Andes mountains almost to the Atlantic, down the length of Argentina and into Chile.

The **Thar Desert** of India and Pakistan once contained fertile river valleys, until a change of wind direction moved the monsoon's path further east some five thousand years ago.

The **Turkestan Desert** has no rain between May and October, and its severe winter frosts kill many animals. It consists of two neighbouring deserts, the Karakum and the Kyzylkum.

The dune forming against this scrubby bush in Death Valley, California, may eventually grow to bury it. Death Valley is the hottest, driest place in North America.

What Happens In A Desert?

A desert is always on the move. Even if it is not spreading, there is constant movement and change within a desert, caused by winds and moving particles of sand and earth. The desert's extremes of hot and cold can split rocks apart, letting the wind in to batter and re-shape them.

ONE OF THE most powerful forces shaping any desert is the wind. Hot winds in the Sahara regularly reach 100 kph. These winds blow away loose material such as flakes loosened by intense heat and frost, and carve and polish rock surfaces with sand grains like a giant sand-blasting machine.

The wind cannot pick up sand grains, but it can roll them along the ground. If they are rolling fast enough, sand grains bounce up into the air when one grain bumps into another. Once in the air, they are blown along by the wind before they fall to the ground again.

The dark and choking 'sand storms' that occur in deserts are actually dust storms. Dust particles are much smaller than sand grains, and they can be blown thousands of metres into the sky. But blown sand stays low. You could sit in a chair and see over a sand storm if there were no dust particles.

Desert winds can clear sand from large areas, leaving boulders and pebbles behind. The cleared areas are called

Powerful desert winds loaded with mineral particles constantly wear away at rocky surfaces, removing any loose fragments to reshape rocks such as these pinnacles in the Libyan Sahara.

Rows of longitudinal dunes stretch inland from the coast of Namibia across the Namib Desert, in line with the direction of the prevailing wind.

Sand-proofing

Desert workers pile stones round the bases of fence posts and telegraph poles to stop them being worn away by the scouring effect of wind and sand. The 'bouncing' sand usually rises no higher than 50–100 cm above the surface of the desert.

desert pavements. Ancient Peruvians made giant desert pictures by moving the stones to reveal paler soil beneath.

How are sand dunes formed?

Dunes are formed when wind that is carrying blown sand slows down, or meets an obstacle. The sand falls to the ground as a small heap, but it doesn't just sit there. Unless plants grow to bind it, the dune moves across the desert at a rate of up to 15m a year. Sand grains are blown up the back slope and tumble over the front or 'slip face'. Since sand moves from the back to the front, the dune keeps moving in the same direction as the wind.

What are the main types of dune?

The barchan is the most common type of dune. It is crescent-shaped, with its 'horns' pointing downwind. Barchan dunes can reach a length of 350m. The rather similar parabolic dunes are also 'horned', but their long horns point into the wind rather than away from it.

Transverse dunes lie at right-angles to the wind, and occur where there is plenty of sand but little vegetation. Some transverse dunes in the Sahara are 100 km long. Longitudinal dunes occur where wind blows from two directions. They lie in line with the prevailing wind, and may be 90m high.

Is there water in the desert?

Deserts are the driest places on the planet, but despite this they are shaped more by water than by wind. Water is a very powerful force, and an occasional rainstorm may have more effect on the landscape than months of wind.

A desert may go without rain for years, then suddenly get a year's supply all at once. When these rainstorms strike, flash floods rush like miniature tidal waves along dry watercourses carved by similar floods over thousands of years. These stream beds, which are usually bone-dry, are called 'arroyos' in America, and 'wadis' in North Africa. Fed by rainwater cascading off the hills and rocks above, each flood bears a heavy load of debris. The water is thick with silt, fractured shale, sand, gravel and rocks. Even large boulders are trundled along the arroyo bottom by the force of the flood.

After a desert downpour the landscape is changed. The water soon disappears, evaporated by the fierce sun. But at the base of the hills, spreading wedges of muddy earth and gravel dry out into 'alluvial fans'. The waterless arroyos have new sandbanks and new boulders. Within hours, seeds that have been dormant for years are sprouting.

The Great Salt Lake

The Great Salt Lake of Utah in the USA is a large playa lake, 112 km long and 48 km wide, sitting in the middle of its own desert, and surrounded by mountains. The lake is so salty that if you bathe in it you cannot sink — but you come out of the water covered in a layer of stinging salt crystals.

Surrounded by a desert of salt flats, Utah's Great Salt Lake supports a number of salt-resistant animals, including the brine shrimp.

Life-supporting desert oases may be small, based on a single spring, but some ribbon-shaped oases in the Sahara extend for 80 km or more.

In uplands, if there are no watercourses leading towards the sea, the storm water may accumulate to form an enclosed 'playa' lake. Year after year, silt-laden water flows into the lake and evaporates, leaving minerals and salts behind. Over time the lake water becomes saturated with the minerals and salts, which make the water completely undrinkable.

What is an oasis?

Many travellers owe their lives to the oases that exist in some deserts. Oases are formed when winds gouge deep troughs in low-lying areas, and expose underground water supplies that fell as rain in prehistoric times. The water that quenches the thirst of oasis visitors could be as much as 20 000 years old. The best known of these 'fossil waters' is a huge supply, estimated to be 150 000 cubic km in volume, that lies beneath the eastern Sahara, and is shared by Egypt, Libya, Chad and the Sudan.

Oases are so vital to the economy of the desert that they often have walls to keep out the sand, and may be planted with date palms and fruit trees.

How Can Life Exist In A Desert?

Deserts usually seem empty and hostile to life, but they are home to a wide range of extremely successful plants and animals. These do not just cling to life. They flourish, in their own way, in some of the harshest environments on Earth.

ALL PLANTS NEED water. Without water, plants wilt, shrivel and finally die. So how do desert plants survive in regions where it may not rain for years? They have solved the moisture problem by evolving in two main ways. They are either drought resisters, or drought evaders.

How do drought resisters survive?

Drought resisters either store water, find it underground, or are able to survive on very small amounts of it. They are perennials – plants which live and grow slowly, sometimes for many years.

The cacti of the American deserts store water in their stems and branches. Many have deeply ridged and folded surfaces. When rain falls, cacti such as the giant saguaro suck up huge quantities of water through their wide-spreading, shallow roots. Most of the rain seeps only a few centimetres into the ground. As the water moves up the stem, the

Yucca plants are able to flourish in the gleaming gypsum sands of the White Sands region of the Chihuahua Desert, where their flowers are pollinated by yucca moths.

Many desert plants, such as these flanking a normally dry stream bed in the Namib Desert, grow to maturity and burst into flower within days of being soaked by a rare rainstorm.

Prickly defences

Plants are eaten by animals, and are often the only source of moisture for much of the year. So like many other desert dwellers, they need to reduce the chances of being eaten by hungry, thirsty neighbours. This is why many desert plants have fearsome arrays of spikes, spines, thorns and prickles.

folds between the ridges open up to make room. Some big cacti can store hundreds of litres of water.

Desert trees often send down long roots to reach underground water supplies. The mesquites of the American deserts – and the acacias of deserts in Africa and elsewhere – have roots that extend up to 50m beneath the desert surface.

Some plants use fat roots called tubers as water tanks. The tuber of the Namibian elephant foot yam can swell with water until it weighs 300 kg or more. Another Namib Desert plant, the welwitschia, has only two leaves, which snake and curl over the ground for up to

20m. Dew collected on these leaves is funnelled into the ground to be stored in the plant's large root.

How do drought evaders survive?

Those desert plants which are drought-evaders are annuals – plants that grow from seed, flower, produce seed and then die all in the space of a few weeks. The seeds of these plants may lie dormant underground for ten years or more until the right conditions, usually rainwater, set them off on a rush of activity. Many of these drought-evaders have brilliant flowers, to attract the insects that pollinate them as quickly as possible before the blazing sun shrivels them.

How do cold-blooded creatures survive in the desert?

'Cold-blooded' animals, which include reptiles, insects and spiders, all have body temperatures that rise and fall with the temperature of their surroundings. This makes burning desert heat as much of a problem for them as freezing cold.

Because of this, many desert creatures are most active in the early morning, evening and night, and rest in the shade or in burrows during the heat of the day.

Many desert animals only become active after rare desert rainstorms. The rains are a busy hatching time for insects and other small animals, because their eggs hatch only if they come into contact with water, just like the seeds of desert plants. Eggs can lie dormant for years. In Australia, freshwater shrimps have appeared in puddles after the first rain in 25 years – having hatched from eggs that have been buried since the last rainstorm. Many insects have short, fast lifecycles like annual plants, passing through all the stages of their lives – hatching, feeding, mating, laying eggs and dying – in a few weeks while the desert is still green from the last rains.

Desert insects get a lot of moisture from their food, whether vegetable or animal, but they may also find unusual ways of drinking. A Namibian darkling beetle obtains water from sea-mist. The beetle stands with its head down and its rear held high at the top of a coastal sand dune. The mist condenses on its wing cases, then trickles down into its mouth.

The thorny devil lizard of the Australian deserts stays active in heat that drives most creatures underground, and hunts ants even in the hottest part of the day.

Like some other desert snakes, the American sidewinder rattlesnake moves normally over firm ground, but loops its body sideways over loose, sandy surfaces.

Although the highest recorded desert air temperature is 58°C, the desert floor regularly reaches surface temperatures of around 80°C in summer. Close contact with this sort of heat could kill most animals in minutes. Some reptiles, including most geckos, avoid the heat altogether by being active only at night. Many spend the hottest part of the day in burrows. Others 'swim' through sand beneath the surface, where it is cooler, as they hunt their insect prey.

Reptiles in deserts in different parts of the world have found similar solutions to the problems of desert life. Moving over a loose sandy surface is difficult for a snake, and the sidewinder viper of the Namib Desert copes with this by moving sideways over the sand, looping its body in a series of S-shapes.

American sidewinder rattlesnakes and Saharan sidewinder adders use exactly the same method.

Air conditioning

A species of Nigerian termite builds towering mounds 7.5m tall. These contain fungus gardens, nurseries for baby termites, and a basement air-conditioning unit which keeps the interior of the mound cool by evaporating water on narrow blades of hardened mud.

How do warm-blooded animals survive in the desert?

Birds and mammals are warm-blooded, which means that they make heat inside their bodies. This is a great advantage in a cold climate, but the birds and mammals that live in hot deserts need ways of getting rid of some of that internal heat.

One way is to use radiators: large panels that give off heat. The big ears of mammals such as fennec foxes and jackrabbits work like this. They have many small blood vessels, and the blood passing through them is cooled as its heat radiates into the air. The thinly-furred belly of a camel radiates heat in the same way.

Long legs are a big advantage in the desert, because the heat is fiercest at ground level. Gazelles and camels have long legs, and the air temperature around a camel's body can be 25°C lower than the temperature around its feet.

Some desert mammals rely on sweating to keep cool. As the sweat evaporates, it draws heat from the animal's skin, making it cooler. Unfortunately the moisture lost by sweating has to be replaced by water. A human in the desert can lose a litre of moisture every hour, and would be dead by the end of the day without water to drink.

Surprisingly, a thick coat of fur is a real benefit in the desert, because it insulates an animal against the intense heat of the sun. A camel has a thick coat on its back – but not on its belly – which keeps its skin relatively cool. This reduces the amount of moisture lost through sweating, and because the camel does not sweat so much, it does not need to

The tiny fennec fox of the Sahara uses its huge ears both to listen out for prey and to help radiate heat away from its body.

The southern African gemsbok sweats to help it stay cool, and gets moisture from bulbs and melons when free water is not available.

drink so much. Camels are famous for their ability to go for long periods without water when not working – for two months or more in winter, and over two weeks in summer.

A camel also saves body moisture by not sweating until its body temperature exceeds 40.5°C. If you allowed your body temperature to rise this far, you would be hospitalized with sunstroke. Camels, and the saiga antelope of the Asian steppes, also have specially constructed noses which reduce the loss of moisture in their breath. Another life-saving feature of a camel is its hump, which stores fat, not water. The camel's body breaks the fat down into energy

and a small amount of water. Fat-tailed mice use the same system in the Australian outback.

Birds can be successful desert dwellers, because their feathers are very good heat barriers. Even so, many birds stay in the shade during the heat of the day. The burrowing owl of the Chihuahua Desert in Mexico avoids the worst of the heat by staying underground during the day, and the elf owl of the nearby Sonoran Desert roosts in well-insulated holes in giant saguaro cacti. African and Asian sandgrouse use their breast feathers as sponges to soak up water, which they often carry long distances to their chicks.

How Can People Survive In Deserts?

The way of life of the last true desert dwellers is coming to an end, but some of the ancient peoples who make the desert their home still survive. They include some of the last humans that live entirely by hunting and gathering plants. Others are tent-living herders, who are always on the move.

PEOPLE HAVE BEEN living in the deserts of the world for thousands of years. In that time they have become experts at survival in these hostile regions. Some of the most expert are the Australian Aborigines, the Kalahari Bushmen, and the Bedouin of Arabia.

The first human colonists reached Australia from Asia at least 40 000 years ago, and some became desert dwellers. The last of these aboriginal groups to be discovered, half-way through the twentieth century, had no houses and no clothes – in fact they had no possessions at all beyond their stone hunting weapons and the tools they used to gather plant food. What they did have was an enormous knowledge, built up over 40 000 years, of food plants, medicine plants, and the ways of the desert and the animals they hunted.

The Bushmen of the Kalahari Desert have been hunting game, collecting plants and surviving the savage heat of the sun for 20 000 years or so. They are probably the world's greatest hunters, able to tell from a footprint if the animal they are following is male or female, sick

The few San Bushmen who still live in their traditional way in Namibia's Kalahari Desert often travel great distances on foot in pursuit of game.

or healthy, young or old. Their way of life is harsh, but they are skilled survivors. They drink water stored by living plants, and cover themselves in sand during the heat of the day. Out in the desert they live in temporary shelters, but most of them have now been forced to leave their hunting territories and live on reservations.

The Bedouin of the Arabian Desert are nomads, and live in tents. They often travel hundreds of kilometres with their flocks, their camels, their families and their tents between grazing areas and oases. A Bedouin tent is made from camel or goat hair, and is wide and low to the ground. Outside the tent, the Bedouin wrap themselves from head to toe in their robes and headdresses. This protects them from the dust storms of the desert, and saves their skin from the blazing sun. The Bedouin depend entirely on their camels, drinking their milk, using their skins and hair for their tents, and burning their dung as fuel.

The yurt of a Mongolian herding family in the Gobi Desert is a portable house, which can be dismantled and carried on horseback to the next grazing site.

DEBATE - Should desert peoples be moved onto reservations?

- Yes. Their desert life is too harsh, causing many to die young. On reservations they can have modern shelter, food and medicine.
- No. Many of them prefer their unique desert life, and reservation life destroys their communities and culture.

How Do Deserts Benefit People?

For centuries most people thought deserts were useless – no good for growing crops, too hot for cattle, and too dry to live in, apart from a few wandering shepherds and their flocks. Then many deserts were found to be treasure-houses of valuable minerals including oil, uranium, and even diamonds.

IN THE TWENTIETH century, with the vast increase in numbers of cars and trucks, petroleum oil became the world's most important fuel. The first oil wells were in the USA, but before long the oil companies discovered that the biggest oil supplies were under the deserts of North Africa and the Middle East. Suddenly many desert kingdoms, where wealth was once measured in camels and sheep, became fabulously rich in oil dollars.

The demand for oil grew at a great speed. New factories and transport systems, including trains, ships and aircraft depended on it. Oil took over from coal as a heating fuel. Natural gas, often

Middle Eastern oilfields, such as this one in Kuwait, produce a large proportion of the world's oil from beneath their desert sands.

This uranium mine in the Namib Desert produces a fuel that can be used in nuclear power stations to generate domestic electricity.

found along with oil, took over from coal gas. Oil was also used in the manufacture of plastics, a gigantic new industry.

More and more desert countries were discovered to have underground oil just waiting to be drilled and pumped. The countries exporting oil formed an organization to help them get the best price for their 'desert gold'. The Organization of Petroleum Exporting Countries (OPEC) included Algeria, Iran, Iraq, Kuwait, Libya, Nigeria, Qatar, Saudi Arabia and the United Arab Emirates – all desert countries.

What other minerals are there in deserts?

Uranium, which is used in the nuclear industry, is another mineral that can be used to generate energy. Like oil, it is difficult and expensive to get out of the ground, and it too has been found in desert sites. Desert uranium mines have been worked in New Mexico, Wyoming and Texas in the USA, as well as in southern Africa and Australia. Asian desert sites include Turkmenistan and the Gobi Desert.

For centuries Saudi Arabia was famous for the gold, silver and copper that were mined from beneath the sand. New mineral searches are revealing more of these metals, plus tin, tungsten, nickel, chrome, zinc, lead, phosphorus, iron, uranium, bauxite and potassium. Valuable minerals mined in other deserts include diamonds in South Africa and Namibia, silver in Mexico, and copper in Chile's Atacama Desert.

DEBATE - Should uranium mining be encouraged in the desert?

- Yes. Unlike oil, nuclear energy is unlikely to run out, and it does not cause global warming.

- No. Uranium is a radioactive poison that has ruined the health of many miners. Also, nuclear accidents such as Chernobyl can affect the lives of thousands of people.

The rapid evaporation caused by desert heat also produces large quantities of minerals. These dissolve in the water that flows from rock layers and soils when it rains, then reappear in mineral form when the water evaporates. They include salt, borax, nitrates and phosphates. Chile has the world's largest known deposits of nitrate in the Atacama Desert. The largest phosphate deposits are in Western Sahara in North Africa. Nitrates and phosphates are used in fertilizers, which help crops grow.

Ordinary people can benefit from all this wealth if the money reaches them in the form of health care, power supplies and

Huge excavators and trucks are used to load copper ore scooped from open-cast mines in Chile's Atacama Desert.

Workers tend a pipeline carrying water that has been pumped from far beneath the surface of a South American desert.

jobs. Everything depends on the price of the mineral staying high. Silver and copper both suffered severe price drops in the late twentieth century, and mining operations were reduced.

Are minerals the only desert resources?

One desert resource that lies deep beneath the surface is not a mineral at all. It is water. In Libya the fossil water beneath the eastern Sahara is being used in a mammoth project to bring water to the cities and irrigate the desert. Spending billions of oil dollars, the Libyan Government began its Great Man-Made River project in 1987. A thousand wells were drilled, and 5000 km of concrete pipe were buried in the desert. By 1994, two million tonnes of fresh water a day were flowing into

Benghazi on the Mediterranean. By 1996 the water was supplying the capital, Tripoli. Bringing the water to farms and factories will take an estimated further ten years and cost 30 billion dollars.

One plentiful resource that has not yet been used to the full is sunshine. For many years it has been possible to generate electricity from light-sensitive solar cells. Most hand-held electronic calculators are powered by them. In Saudi Arabia solar cells are set up on remote desert roads to power emergency telephones and electric signs. The Saudi authorities have even equipped several villages with electric power systems working off solar cells, and have used them in experimental machines to remove the salt from sea water.

Can Human Activity Create Deserts?

*None of the world's major deserts were created by humans.
A true desert is a natural system – and desert life, from
plants to large mammals, has adapted to the conditions.
But unlike true deserts, the degraded, arid land often created
by human activities is practically lifeless.*

ABOUT TEN THOUSAND years ago, people began to abandon their life of nomadic herding and change to a more settled life as farmers. They cultivated crops and raised livestock on the Mesopotamian plain between two great rivers, the Euphrates and the Tigris, roughly where modern Iraq lies. The land was rich with river silt from regular flooding.

The early farmers grew wheat and flourished. First villages, then cities grew up on the plain between the rivers. Between seasonal floods, the land baked hard as rock, particularly in the south, so the farmers irrigated their fields with river water. But most of the water came from the slow-flowing Euphrates, which was saltier than the faster Tigris. They used too much of it, and carried on

Overgrazing has stripped the vegetation in many Middle Eastern countries, leading to erosion that exposes the barren bedrock.

A dust storm gets underway on the Oklahoma Plain in the 1930s. Such storms removed huge quantities of exhausted topsoil from the Dust Bowl of the American Midwest.

DEBATE - Should crops be planted in areas liable to suffer drought?

- Yes. People need food, and the land can be revived by replacing nutrients and letting it rest periodically.
- No. These areas need drought-resistant wild plants that hold the soil together with their roots.

doing so for thousands of years. The soil became choked with salt, and eventually – from a combination of over-irrigation, drought and neglect due to frequent local wars – the land could no longer support plants. It had become more barren than any natural desert.

What is a dust bowl?

In the Great Plains states of North America's wheat belt, ancient grasslands with earth-gripping root systems were ploughed up so the farmers could plant wheat and other crops. The crops were grown and harvested, year after year, without replacing the nutrients taken from the soil. The land was literally worked to death. The starved topsoil turned to dust, and the wind carried it away.

The worst-affected area of the Midwestern states became known as the Dust Bowl. In the 1930s the wind began to strip away the topsoil of the whole region. Skies turned as black as night, as millions of tonnes of dusty earth were carried eastwards and dumped far out in the Atlantic.

The Dust Bowl of the 1930s was created by a combination of exhausted soil and unusually low rainfall. Such natural droughts occur roughly every twenty years on the Great Plains. After 1939 the land began to recover, thanks to increased rainfall and greater soil care. Some areas of original prairie have even been restored by planting drought-resistant grasses. Low rainfall between 1955 and 1957 brought the dust storms back, but with less damage.

Since the trees which once formed a protective barrier were felled, sand and dust blowing in from the Gobi Desert have become a major health hazard for the inhabitants of Beijing.

Will Beijing disappear beneath the sands?

In China, an average of 2460 sq. km of land deteriorates into desert every year. China lies in the wind-path of the Gobi Desert, and years of deforestation to expand farmland have removed the barrier of trees that once held back the desert storms. Nearly one million tonnes of sand blow into Beijing each year. Most of the grass has disappeared from the once-fertile valleys north of the capital, and has been replaced by moving sand dunes. The sand destroys the food plots of corn, rice, beans and tomatoes which keep the villagers alive.

Scientists are warning that Beijing may be silted over in a few years. In the

1950s dust storms reached Beijing once every seven or eight years. By the 1990s they had become a yearly problem. In 2000, ferocious dust storms closed Beijing airport, and filled the hospitals with people suffering from breathing problems. In the second week of March 2002, sand storms engulfed north and northwest China, triggered by sudden spring temperature changes. Sand dunes are forming only 70 km from the capital, and may be drifting south at up to 25 km each year.

The Chinese government has begun a tree-planting project called 'China's Great Green Wall', to take place over the next 70 years, and villagers have been signed up for the 'green army'. However, no one knows what to do with the sand.

What happens when the firewood runs out?

In the countries of the Sahel, along the southern fringes of the Sahara, firewood is being used up at least 30 per cent faster than it is being produced. New tree growth cannot keep up with the firewood collectors.

In Niger, one of the Sahel countries, wood is the main fuel for over 90 per cent of all households. Two million tonnes of firewood are burned every year, and it all has to be collected either in farming areas or in the 'green belt' areas south of the Sahara.

Villagers find themselves competing with teams of firewood collectors from the towns, who travel in trucks up to 300 km from home in search of wood. The dead wood was finished long ago, and now living trees and bushes are cut down. When they die, the soil around their roots is easily stripped away by the harsh Sahara winds.

In western Sudan some villages are threatened by sand dunes which reach roof height. The Sahara is only 200 km away, but these dunes are formed from soil in the farming territories, which has crumbled and blown away because the trees that once held it in place have been cut down for firewood.

A guard looks after a firewood store in Burkina Faso, where, as in other Sahel countries, burning far exceeds wood production.

Why did the Aral Sea shrink?

The Aral Sea of Central Asia was once the fourth largest lake in the world, with an area of 68 000 sq. km. Fed by two rivers, it had a flourishing fishing industry and a busy shipping trade. But in the 1960s huge new irrigation schemes for cotton plantations took 90 per cent of the waters flowing into the Aral Sea. The Sea began to shrink rapidly. The salt content of the water increased. The fish began to die, and by the early 1980s the fishermen had all lost their jobs. The new crops of cotton and rice were treated with enormous quantities of pesticides, which drained back into the rivers, and so into the Aral Sea.

By the 1990s, the surface of the Aral Sea had shrunk by a half, and its water volume was down by 75 per cent. The exposed seabed is thick with salt and pesticides. Every day strong winds carry thousands of tonnes of the dusty, poisonous mixture over the surrounding countryside, where it destroys crops and grazing land. The people who used to work on and around the Sea suffer terrible illnesses through breathing in the dust. Aral Sea dust storms have even been reported as far away as the Arctic.

The huge size of the Aral Sea disaster has had an effect on the local weather.

Boats which once sailed the waters of Kazakhstan's Aral Sea are now permanently stranded, since excessive irrigation for water-thirsty cotton crops has caused the great lake to shrink and dry up.

Satellite images of the Aral Sea region show that the giant lake is getting smaller every year, exposing large areas of former lake bed.

There is less rainfall, and the growing season is shorter. Meanwhile, the Sea continues to shrink.

How do you feed a growing population?

Mongolia is a large but poor country, and its small population is growing at the rate of 1.8 per cent each year. Three-quarters of the country consists of semi-desert grasslands on which nomadic herders graze their flocks and herds. There is little other agriculture.

As the population grows in the towns, where 64 per cent of Mongols live, there is strong pressure to increase the size of the flocks and herds to help feed the extra mouths. The country now has 25 million grazing animals, far more than the land and traditional grazing methods can cope with.

Overgrazing has ruined some traditional herding regions, and sand has overtaken the tough grasses that the animals eat. Drought and over-use has dried up many of the wells, and some herders have had to leave the land. In places people have attempted to increase food-producing land by cutting down trees and ploughing the thin desert soils. The results are disastrous, exposing fragile soil to extreme temperatures and strong winds.

What Is Desertification?

True deserts are formed naturally over thousands of years, but desert conditions created by humans develop much faster. Ploughing, firewood collection or overgrazing can transform a vulnerable area of drought-prone terrain into a barren wasteland within a decade.

FOR TENS OF thousands of years the Sahara region had a wet climate. Saharan rock paintings and engravings ranging over a period of 8000 years show men harvesting grain and herding cattle. They also show wild animals such as giraffes and hippos.

The region where the pictures are found was fertile grassland for thousands of years, but after the Ice Age, about 12 000 years ago, it began to dry out. Gradually, as rainfall and wind patterns changed, it became true desert. Today it has an average rainfall of only 100 mm per year.

Like other true deserts, the Sahara contains animals and plants that have had thousands of years to adapt to the heat and scarce moisture. The desert-like regions created accidentally by humans have happened quickly, often within a

An ancient rock engraving from what is now an Algerian desert portrays a time when herders could graze their cattle there.

Where land has been ruined by overgrazing, by the growing of inappropriate crops, and by the destruction of trees, a drought can cause a catastrophe. Both people and livestock die of thirst and starvation.

few years, and neither plants nor animals have had time to adapt. They die out or leave, so the 'artificial deserts' really are barren. They can recover if the rains return, but meanwhile they are almost lifeless.

How can people create deserts so quickly?

For centuries the peoples of the Sahel region south of the Sahara had existed by herding cattle, growing crops and vegetables in village plots, and hunting. But in the twentieth century, the governments of Sahel nations urged their people to grow single crops, such as peanuts and millet, to earn money from exports. Vegetable plots and grazing areas were cleared for the new crops. The herders moved their animals further north towards the Sahara, into drier areas with less vegetation.

The cattle became less healthy because there were too many of them for the scarce food in the dry territories. The new crops weakened the soil, which began to be blown away by the wind. As populations increased, people started cutting down living trees for firewood, removing wind barriers. And just when the people and their animals were at their weakest, the Sahel was struck by a savage drought. The combination of natural and man-made disasters cost thousands of human lives and millions of animal lives.

The Sahel drought was at its worst in the mid-1970s. By the 1980s the rains were returning, and satellite pictures taken in the 1990s were showing new growth of both wild vegetation and crops. But the droughts could return, and the story shows just how easy it is to create a desert by bad land management.

Raked out

In Chinese Inner Mongolia, tens of thousands of square kilometres of semi-arid grazing lands have been destroyed by gangs of poor farmers from outside the region. They use rakes to harvest *facai* grasses, destroying other plants in the process. The word *facai* means 'get rich' in Chinese, and the grasses are sold at high prices as good-luck charms.

What causes desertification?

The process starts with the loss of natural plant cover. Trampled by cattle, destroyed to make room for saleable crops, chopped down for firewood, gnawed down to the roots, the plants that protect the soil disappear. The earth is crushed by heavy tractors, repeatedly ploughed, laced with pesticides and fertilizers, crusted with irrigation salts, and sucked dry by quick-growing cash crops. Soil surfaces become baked, then crumble. Natural events, such as flash floods, sudden storms or strong winds, which the land would have comfortably survived before the loss of the plants, finish the job off. The topsoil departs. Every year about 24 000 million tonnes of topsoil are stripped from the planet's surface like this. It is possible to reverse the process, and heal the damaged land, but that requires time and care.

Are developed countries at risk too?

Australia is the world's driest continent after Antarctica, and agriculture occupies 60 per cent of the total land area. Most Australian farmers are livestock raisers, and about half the total land area is used for grazing. Huge amounts of water are needed to support the sheep flocks and cattle herds, and because of this, Australia uses more water per person than any other country in the world.

Fertile lands once covered much of Jordan, but many shepherds now tend their flocks on poor, rocky terrain with sparse plant cover.

Huge areas of Australia are devoted to sheep farming, but the flocks need access to plentiful water supplies. The harsh droughts that strike some regions can spell disaster for some sheep farmers and their animals.

Since the arrival of Europeans, about half the country has had its vegetation either cleared or thinned to make way for livestock ranching. Most Australian soils are shallow, salty and low in plant foods. They are easily damaged by overgrazing, and by the hooves of animals milling around artificial watering ponds. Trampled and compressed, the soils lose their plant cover. The root systems of grasses are destroyed, and the soils turn to dust under the hot sun.

Cattle ranchers often cram more cattle onto some ranges than the land can support, to try and make up the money lost by having underweight animals. But if more cattle have to share the same pasture, they just get even thinner. Many cattle ranchers have lost everything due to this short-sighted policy, and have been forced to abandon their ruined ranges.

DEBATE - Should ranchers clear natural vegetation to make cattle ranges?

- Yes. Cattle provide food and money from exports, and wild country is unproductive.

- No. Cleared land often has easily damaged soils which end up supporting neither cattle nor natural plants, and can become desert.

What Is Happening To The Desert Wildlife?

When a large herd animal virtually disappears we take notice, but desertification also destroys the small creatures which live at the bottom of the food chain. Without them, nothing else can survive for long, and with no animals to recycle nutrients, the land cannot grow healthy plants.

THE ADDAX IS a type of antelope that is more highly adapted to life in the desert than any of it relatives. It can exist on a diet of tough grasses, and hardly ever has to drink. When no grass is available, it browses on spiny acacia bushes and herbs. It wanders great distances, mainly at night or in the early morning, seeking food. At the beginning of the twentieth century addax ranged over 8 million sq. km of the Sahara region. Now it is one of the world's rarest mammals, relentlessly hunted for meat, and no longer able to compete with the ever-growing herds of domestic animals.

The addax is able to survive where most other animals would die of thirst, but now faces extinction throughout its range.

The Australian bilby is a small burrowing marsupial that only comes out at night. It was once common, but predators and competitors introduced by settlers have reduced its numbers to dangerously low levels.

The African wild ass has also been reduced to a few small herds. It once wandered stony deserts and semi-arid bush from Morocco in the west to Arabia in the east. Now a few small herds hang on along the shores of the Red Sea. Its main problem is competition with domestic cattle and sheep for food and water. It has also been driven off or killed by the herders, who want the food and water for their livestock.

What about the smaller animals?

Large desert mammals are among the most obvious victims of desertification, but the process creates many less visible casualties. Insect grubs, worms and other tiny creatures live in the soil itself. They keep the soil in good condition by breaking down dead plants and animal waste into plant food. They also provide food for lizards, birds and small mammals. If these small animals cannot survive, then neither can the larger predators that feed on them, such as hawks, foxes and wild cats.

When desertification is accompanied by increases in salt and poisonous minerals in the earth, due to excess irrigation, this also affects the water in wells and water holes. Anything that depends on these water sources, from toads and snakes to gazelles and zebras, either dies out or has to move elsewhere.

What other threats face desert wildlife?

As well as having their habitats cleared by farmers and destroyed by cattle and sheep, many smaller animals in Australia have declined in numbers because of introduced animals. The invaders either eat them, or compete with them for food. Cats, foxes and rabbits are among the main problems. One casualty is the bilby, a rabbit-like creature that eats seeds, fruits and bulbs as well as insects and spiders. It has fallen drastically in numbers, and its relative the desert bandicoot has become extinct.

Habitat clearance by farmers leaves such small mammals nowhere to hide, and they are easily picked off by predators. Both the fox and the rabbit were introduced to Australia to be hunted for sport, but both have multiplied in numbers to become major pests – and threats to native species.

Is hunting a problem too?

Desertification and poverty are closely linked, because poor villagers are more interested in providing food for their families than in conservation. In the Sahara and Sahel countries many animals are hunted ruthlessly. In Mauritania, which has suffered severe desertification, ostriches, dama gazelles and oryx have been hunted almost to extinction by hungry villagers.

The same thing is happening in the Gobi Desert of Mongolia – home of some of the planet's most endangered animals. Many are killed illegally so the hunters can sell their body parts to Asian medicine dealers. The victims

Mass slaughter

In 1991 the Ethiopian president was toppled from power. He had been a cruel leader, but he looked after wildlife very well, setting up several national parks. After the revolution poor villagers swarmed into the parks, along with their cattle, and began slaughtering the wildlife with Kalashnikov sub-machine guns. Many of the parks are now suffering desertification, and some people estimate that within ten years Ethiopia will have no wildlife left.

In several countries, rare or supposedly protected wild animals are regularly killed, not for local food, but for the international trade in skins, ivory and body parts.

include musk deer, brown bears, saiga antelope, argali mountain sheep, elk and snow leopards.

Mali is one of many African countries where overgrazing by domestic cattle has destroyed the plants that wild animals need for food and shelter.

Desert life is harsh. Wild animals compete with one another, and humans and their cattle are competing for their share. People need food, and the wildlife they hunt often provides them with nourishing meat. The herder's cattle also need food and water. But it is not an equal competition. Cattle need more water than wild animals, and they destroy many of the plants that the wild animals eat. The herders would probably be better off in the long run if they tried to look after the land and grew a variety of food plants, but most of them know no other life.

DEBATE - Should wild animals be protected when local people are going hungry?

- Yes. Small populations of wild animals are soon wiped out by hunting, and may even become extinct.
- No. People are more important than animals, and wild animals do not belong to anybody.

How Are We Addressing The Problems?

Desertification cannot be cured in a few days. To halt it and repair the damage takes knowledge and patience. Huge tree-planting schemes or heavy irrigation projects can make things worse. We are beginning to realize that the answer might be to cure it nature's way – slowly but surely.

THE BEST WAY to stop a dune moving or blowing away is to plant it with dune grasses or desert bushes. But how do you hold the dune still while the grasses are taking root? In oil-producing Iran, where over 80 per cent of the land is arid or semi-arid, they spray a layer of crude oil sludge over the dune. This holds the sand steady and keeps moisture in. Seedlings are planted through the oil layer. The system seems to be working, and many farms have been set up in the dune-planting region.

Have other schemes been equally successful?

China has 1.65 million sq. km of deserts and desertified land. Over 22 per cent of this wasteland has been created by

A Moroccan worker builds low barriers from palm fronds to stabilize dunes, and stop the sand moving into agricultural land.

A Palestinian farmer checks the drip-irrigation system which delivers precise amounts of water to the roots of young plants.

human activities. Erosion rates have risen from 1560 sq. km per year in the 1970s to 3436 sq. km per year in the late 1990s. Worried about the sandy dust storms bringing the desert into Beijing, the Chinese government planted a huge barrier of trees across the north of the country to keep out the sands of Inner Mongolia. But the project was an expensive failure, because 1200 km of the shelter-belt withered and died from lack of water.

Chinese scientists came to the conclusion that the sandstorms were coming from the human-created desert areas, and not from the true desert. They fenced off areas to be restored, stopped all cultivation and grazing, and sowed the ground from the air with drought-resistant grasses and shrubs. After four

to five years, 40–60 per cent of the test areas were covered in vegetation. The erosion was stopped by allowing nature's self-repair system a chance to work.

The Negev Desert covers 60 per cent of Israel. When rain does fall, the eroded hills funnel it straight down into low-lying areas and wadis. By placing walled terraces in the lowlands, ancient farmers were able to use the run-off water for crops. Modern Negev farmers are combining these ancient terracing methods with modern drip-irrigation, which enables them to use poor-quality water by delivering it to the roots rather than the leaves of plants. The combination of ancient and modern techniques allows them to grow a wide range of crops, including barley, wheat, olives, figs and pistachios.

Dogon women carry freshly harvested millet, a staple food in Sahelian countries, grown for local consumption and as a cash crop.

What types of plants are needed?

Like many crops, millet is an annual plant. It springs from a seed, grows tall, flowers, develops seeds, and dies all in one year. The seeds fall into the ground, or are carried off by birds, and become plants themselves in one or more years, when moisture makes them sprout.

Other plants are known as perennials. Their foliage may die back each year, but it returns the next season, and the plant gets bigger and stronger from year to year. In the wild, perennials such as trees and bushes hold the soil together with their roots, and protect it from erosion by wind or water. They protect the wild annual plants at the same time, and enrich the ground with their fallen leaves and fruits.

Throughout the countries of the Sahel, in Africa, the land has been cleared of its natural cover by slashing and burning to make room for annual crops that can be sold for cash. Perennial plants have been dug up, so the annual crops have to grow without their protection. The Sahara winds kill the seedlings and keep the surviving plants small. The topsoil becomes eroded, and threatened with desertification.

One of the most effective ways of halting desertification and restoring the land to fertility is to re-stock it with perennial plants. This is being done successfully in parts of Niger, where 2500 sq. km of land are lost annually to desertification. Since 1988 the Eden Foundation, a non-profit-making organization from Sweden, has been carrying out seeding tests with native perennial plants at its base in Niger. Local villagers have now realized that, with the protection of perennial plants, their crops produce far larger harvests. Useful perennial plants with edible fruits or foliage can be planted beside crop fields, or in strips within the crop fields – providing food, shelter and, eventually, renewable supplies of essential firewood.

The perennials add food to the soil, and wild plants begin to return, providing soil cover to areas of the farming zone, and encouraging the return of wildlife species. Traditional water-saving methods are also being successfully reintroduced in Sahel countries. They include laying lines of stones across slopes, and digging numerous small pits; both allow rainwater to soak into the ground instead of being lost as run-off. The pits are also enriched with manure. So irrigation, artificial chemical fertilizers and pesticides are all unnecessary.

Trees planted at the foot of gigantic Saharan dunes act as a barrier, protecting the crops and grazing areas of a Libyan oasis from the surrounding desert.

What is the role of governments?

The governments of countries where desertification is a problem are keen to do something about it, but they usually tell the farmers what to do instead of consulting them first. These orders from above are often the reason for the problem.

When poor governments borrow money from international banks, the banks often make growing cash crops for export a condition of the loan. So governments eager to borrow money tell their people to grow annual crops such as peanuts and millet, which can be sold as exports. Large areas of perennial plants have been cleared by government schemes to make room for such crops.

Villagers' needs for a variety of food crops that can be harvested throughout the year, and land where they can hunt for game, are not taken into account – and neither is the risk of desertification.

As the extent of desertification has become more visible, local and international organizations have tried to deal with it in a scientific way. In China, where desertification is widespread, the Chinese Academy of Forestry has a Desertification Division which has teamed up with scientists from the United Nations Convention to Combat Desertification (UNCCD). One of their schemes involves the use of orbiting surveyor satellites to provide early warnings of desertification.

Annual cash crops such as peanuts need plenty of water, remove nutrients from the soil, and leave it exposed when they are harvested.

Women in Burkina Faso pack down the earth of an artificial ridge, designed to stop the soil being washed away when the rains come.

The UNCCD was set up in the early 1990s, to help countries with desertification problems, and 179 governments had signed up by March 2002. Its stated aims are to get effective actions going. It wants to link local programmes with support from international partners. It stresses the importance of involving local people. It states 'Desertification can only be reversed through profound changes in local and international behaviour'.

DEBATE - Can the adoption of modern farming methods deal with the problems of desertification?

- Yes. Only modern machines and chemicals can make degraded lands productive, and able to grow enough food to feed the expanding populations.

- No. Small-scale traditional farming has worked for centuries, and is the best way of repairing land damaged by intensive cropping.

Where Do We Go From Here?

Organizations like the UNCCD produce large amounts of information about what causes desertification, and the best ways of dealing with it. However, knowing why something happens and what to do about it does not solve the problem. The theory has to be put into practice.

SOME GOVERNMENTS of arid lands may well be happy to team up with international partners to tackle their desertification. Such organizations can be very useful if they help poor nations to have access to expensive items such as satellites for monitoring weather, and computer programmes that can make long-range forecasts about droughts and land loss.

But they may be less keen to be told their cash crops are ruining the land. Politicians are often unwilling to consult with the villagers, and many of them want to see their countries move away from traditional village life, and towards the sort of lifestyle enjoyed in wealthy nations. Most young village people would probably agree with them.

If grazing and firewood collection go unchecked, arid lands can become more and more degraded until they turn into barren deserts.

By using farming techniques that prevent desertification, village people in arid lands can work towards a secure future.

In the real world, however, such aspirations will not help the millions of people who are suffering from the effects of desertification. These people need simple solutions that address basic problems. For example, the over-collection of firewood has speeded up the destruction. It is now possible to obtain a cheap, efficient stove which burns far less wood, and this reduces the need for firewood.

Another problem is uncontrolled grazing. Effective electric fencing for livestock can be powered by solar energy, making it easy, and cheap, to control the movements of herds. It might also be possible to 'farm' some wild desert animals instead of cattle. Early Egyptian farmers used oryx and addax as domestic animals. Unlike today's cattle, these native species have evolved to survive in desert conditions.

They can thrive on a far rougher diet than domestic cattle, and do less damage to the vegetation. They can also go for long periods without water. Millions of cattle in sub-Saharan Africa die in the major droughts that seem to be happening with increasing frequency, while native species are far less affected.

Education is one of the most powerful tools for fighting desertification. On the global level it is important that children in the developed, industrialized countries learn about the problems faced by children living where desertification is an everyday reality. On the local level, the children of the drylands villages need to understand the basic causes of desertification, and learn to apply the traditional techniques that can nurse degraded soil back to health. Better understanding, at both global and local levels, is essential for success.

REFERENCE

Principal Deserts

Sahara
Northern Africa 9 065 000 sq. km
70% gravel plains, 30% sand

Arabian Desert
Arabian peninsula
2 590 000 sq. km
Gravel plains, rocky highlands, 25%
sand (Empty Quarter)

Great Western Desert
Australia 1 346 800 sq. km
Sandhills, gravel, grass;
contains Ayers Rock monolith

Gobi Desert
Mongolia, China 1 295 000 sq. km
Stony, sandy soil; steppes

Patagonian Desert
Argentina 673 400 sq. km
Gravel plains, plateaus,
basaltic sheets

Turkistan Desert
Turkmenistan, Uzbekhistan
647 500 sq. km
Kara-Kum: 90% grey sand
Kyzyl-Kum: red sand and rock

Kalahari Desert
Southern Africa 569 800 sq. km
Sand-sheets, longitudinal dunes

Great Basin
USA 492 100 sq. km
Mountain ridges and valleys.
1% sand dunes

Chihuahuan Desert
Mexico, S.W. USA 453 200 sq. km
Huge shrub desert with mountains,
basins, playa lakes, quartz and
gypsum dunes

Thar Desert
India, Pakistan 453 200 sq. km
Rocky sand, sand dunes

Colorado Plateau
USA 336 700 sq. km
Mesas and plateaus, including Grand
Canyon

Sonoran Desert
USA, Mexico 310 800 sq. km
Basins, plains bordered by mountain
ridges

Taklamakan Desert
China 271 950 sq. km
Sand, dunes, gravel

Iranian Desert
Iran 259 000 sq. km
Salt, gravel, rock

Atacama Desert
Chile 139 900 sq. km
Salt basins, sand, lava

Mojave Desert
USA 139 900 sq. km
Mountain chains, dry alkaline lake
beds, calcium carbonate dunes

Namib Desert
Southern Africa 33 700 sq. km
Gravel plains, linear sand dunes

DESERTS AND DESERTIFICATION

- Each year 6 million hectares of productive land are lost because of desertification and land degradation.

- United Nations, World Bank and NASA figures show that 30% of irrigated land, 47% of cultivated rain-fed land and 73% of rangeland lose some or all of their produce annually due to land degradation.

- The Food and Agriculture Organization of the UN says that 2% of the entire planet's land area is severely affected by land degradation.

REGIONS AT RISK: AFRICA

- 65% of the African continent consists of deserts and drylands.

- 75% of the agricultural drylands are in the process of desertification.

- Soil erosion is now at a critical level.

- Severe droughts have wrecked harvests through the 1990s.

- Between 1974 and 1990 sub-Saharan African food imports rose 185%, and food aid rose 295%.

(Source: UNCCD/UNEP)

REGIONS AT RISK: ASIA

- Of Asia's total land area of 4.3 billion hectares, 1.7 billion hectares are drylands, either dry-subhumid, semi-arid or arid, from the sands of the Middle East to the eroded mountainsides of Nepal and beyond to the Gobi and northern China.

REGIONS AT RISK: NORTHERN MEDITERRANEAN

- Much of the region is semi-arid, experiencing seasonal droughts.

- Over-tilling and overgrazing for many centuries have helped the land become dry and salinized (salty).

- Forest fires, droughts and floods have also contributed to soil degradation. Many degraded areas have been abandoned.

REGIONS AT RISK: LATIN AMERICA AND THE CARIBBEAN

- About 25% of this region consists of desert and semi-arid land.

- The Pacific coast is mostly desert, the Altiplano of the Andes is a high, dry plain, and east of the Andes the land is desiccated (dried up) from the Chaco to southern Argentina.

- Mexico is mainly arid and semi-arid. Several Caribbean islands have water shortages and erosion in their arid zones.

DESERT OIL SUPPLIES

- In 2001 the Middle East accounted for 65% of the world's proven conventional oil reserves, 30% of all production, and 83% of world excess capacity. It also enjoyed the world's cheapest production costs.

- Much of this oil is imported by the USA and Europe. Relative world imports of crude oil can be judged from these figures for 1997 (millions of tonnes):

USA	398.1
Western Europe	389.1
Other Asia/Pacific	274.3
Japan	233.1
Central Europe	52.5
South/Central America	51.3
Canada	37.9
China	35.5
Australasia	23.3
East/Southern Africa	23.0
Total World	1543.8

(Source: BP Statistical Review of World Energy, 1998)

The quantities of oil imported by these countries is increasing, as indicated by total crude oil imports (in millions of barrels) to the USA:

1990	1995	1999	2000
2151	2639	3187	3320

(Source: US Census Bureau, 2002)

According to the Energy Information Administration, US oil demand is expected to rise by 30%, from an average of 19.7 million barrels a day in 2002, to over 26 million barrels a day in 2020.

POPULATION

- The twentieth century began with a world population of 1.6 billion and ended with 6.1 billion.

- The UN population division calculates that by 2050, world population will have reached 9.3 billion, with the most rapid growth in the least developed countries, where the population will almost triple.

- Overpopulation, high water use and overgrazing are causing desertification in many places.

- Over the next 20 years some 60 million people in North Africa are expected to leave the Sahel region unless desertification is halted.

(Source: Kofi Annan, Secretary-General of the UN, June 17 2002)

WEALTH AND POVERTY

- Desert nations with oil reserves are usually wealthy, while those without are often poverty-stricken. National wealth is often measured as Gross Domestic Product (GDP), which is the value of all goods and services produced domestically. Purchasing power parity (ppp) is a way of calculating incomes in terms of what they can purchase, so that comparisons can be made with other countries.

- Only 1% of the land of Saudi Arabia is fertile, but it has 25% of the world's oil reserves and is the largest oil producer. GDPppp is US$232 billion, which works out at about US$10,500 per head, for a population of 23.5 million.

Life expectancy is 70 years at birth, and infant mortality is about 41 for every 1000 live births.

- Niger, in the Sahel region south of the Sahara, subsists mainly on agriculture, which occupies 90% of the workforce. GDPppp is around US$10 billion, or approximately US$1000 per head for a population of 10.8 million. Approximately 60% of the population are below the poverty line. Life expectancy at birth is just 42 years, and infant mortality is 122 deaths per 1000 live births.

(Source: Family Education Network Inc. 2000–2002; Economist Intelligence Unit, 2003)

- Income in sub-Saharan Africa fell to an average of US$474 per head in the year 2000. Bottom of the list was Ethiopia, with $100. Average life expectancy in sub-Saharan Africa is around 47 years.

(Source: The Daily News, All Africa Global Media, 2003)

ENDANGERED WILDLIFE

Sonoran Desert
Migratory pollinators including lesser long-nosed bats, rufous hummingbirds, and monarch butterflies are affected by habitat destruction. Dependant on them are many of the 195 rare or vulnerable desert plants.The Sonoran desert ironwood tree is now threatened by human activities including the wood-carving industry, firewood collectors and charcoal burners.

(Source: Endangered Species Bulletin, March/June 2002)

Sahara
Large mammals have been reduced by hunting and habitat loss. Especially rare are the addax, down to a few hundred, slender-horned gazelle, dama gazelle, red-fronted gazelle and oryx. Most of the desert antelopes in the region are endangered.

(Source: IUCN 2003; World Wildlife Fund, 2000)

Gobi Desert
Mammals endangered by habitat loss, overgrazing, poaching and illegal trade in animal parts include the snow leopard, Gobi bear and Mongolian saiga antelope.

Kalahari Desert
Brown hyenas are rare owing to persecution by ranchers who believe they kill livestock.

Australian Desert
Many small desert species have been reduced by competition with and predation by introduced species. Dibblers, dusky hopping mice and western barred bandicoots have all become rare.

Turkestan Desert
Agricultural and industrial development, and redistribution of water resources have contributed to the rarity of Indian honey badgers, lynx, goitered gazelles, short-toed eagles, imperial eagles and vultures.

Thar Desert
Poaching, habitat destruction and habitat mismanagement threaten antelopes like the Indian blackbuck, and predators like the caracal. The Indian bustard has been reduced to 600-700 birds.

(Source: Oriental Bird Club)

GLOSSARY

alluvial fan A fan-shaped layer of sand and gravel laid down by water.

annual plant A plant that grows from seed, flowers, produces seeds, then dies, all in one year.

arid Used to describe an area with less than 25 cm of annual rainfall.

arroyo A temporary watercourse in an American desert that fills only after rare rainstorms.

artificial fertilizer Factory-made chemicals used to increase plant growth.

cactus A spiny, water-storing plant found only in the American deserts.

cash crop A crop grown to sell rather than to eat or use on the farm.

cereal A grain crop such as wheat.

climate The average weather in an area over a long period.

cold-blooded animal An animal that must bask in the sun or seek shade to maintain its body temperature.

condensation The process by which a gas or vapour turns into a liquid.

desert An area of very dry land with extremely low average rainfall.

desertification The process by which natural events and human activities reduce fertile land to barren land.

dormant Describes animals or plants in which all life processes have almost stopped, usually until warmth or water wakes them up, sometimes after years.

drought An unusually long period without rain.

dune A hill of sand formed by wind, which sometimes moves in the same direction as the wind.

erosion The wearing away of earth, rock or some other substance by water or wind-borne sand.

evaporation The process by which a liquid such as water turns into a gas such as water vapour.

evolve The process by which living things change over many generations (also evolution).

flash flood A sudden, dramatic flood caused by very heavy rain.

game Wild animals hunted for food by humans.

global warming The heating up of the atmosphere, due in some part to human activities.

gravel A build-up of small stones.

intensive farming Growing the maximum amount of plants or raising the maximum amount of livestock that a plot of land can carry.

irrigation Introducing water to growing plants through channels or pipes.

mineral salts Natural chemicals in the soil, sometimes brought to the surface by over-irrigation.

native plant A wild plant that grows naturally in an area.

nomad A herder who has no fixed home, but moves around with the animals between feeding sites.

oasis A fertile spot in a desert, supplied with underground water.

overgrazing Grazing land for too long, or with too many animals, resulting in the destruction of plant cover and eventual desertification.

perennial A plant that stays growing in the earth for many years.

pesticides Poisonous chemicals used to kill insects, weeds, fungi and other crop pests.

plant nutrients Natural plant foods in the earth.

playa lake A lake in a hot region that has no drainage stream, which collects water that then evaporates in the hot climate.

pollination Carrying pollen from one flower to another, fertilizing it so it sets seed.

precipitation Natural water that falls from the sky in the form of rain, snow, sleet, hail, dew, frost and fog.

predators Animals that kill other animals for food.

radiation Getting rid of heat into the air from a surface.

rangelands Uncultivated lands that are used for grazing livestock.

reservations Areas set aside for native wildlife or peoples.

Sahel The region of semi-arid lands to the south of the Sahara in Africa.

sandstorm A desert dust storm, with sand blowing along near ground level.

shale A rock made from hardened mud.

solar cell A device that uses sunlight to generate electricity.

steppe A dry, grassy plain.

stubble The stalks left above ground after a crop has been harvested.

sunstroke A dangerous condition where the body loses its ability to cool itself down.

topsoil The top layer of the earth, where many of the nutrients are.

transpiration The loss of water vapour from plant leaves.

tuber A water-storing plant root.

wadi A temporary watercourse in a North African or Arabian desert that fills only after rare rainstorms (the same as an American arroyo).

warm-blooded animal An animal that maintains a high body temperature by using up food energy.

water vapour Water in the form of an invisible gas.

FURTHER INFORMATION

BOOKS

Climate Change
by Simon Scoones
(Hodder Wayland, 2001)
Graphic and immediate explanations of
the ways we affect the planet's climate.

The Climate Revealed
by W. J. Burroughs
(Mitchell Beazley, 1999)
Relates weather patterns to the deserts.
Clear explanations and descriptions of
prairies and steppes, El Niño, long-term
weather cycles, desertification, the Sahel
drought, and other climatic topics.

Deserts
by Marco Ferrari
(Swan Hill Press, 1996)
Stunning photographs of the world's
major deserts, including space shuttle
pictures. Good on peoples, animals
and plants.

The Encroaching Desert
by Norman Feather
(Dryad Press, 1990)
A very clear and thorough look at the
processes and problems of
desertification, accessible to all age
groups.

Focus on Earth Science
by Hesser and Leach
(Merrill Publishing Co. 1987)
A clearly illustrated guide, very
accessible to younger readers.

Geology
by Chernicoff and Witney
(Houghton Mifflin, 2002)
Includes a very good section on deserts
and wind action. Includes descriptions
of the American Dust Bowl.

Journey into the Desert
by John Brown
(OUP, 2002)
Graphic accounts of the physical
experience of visiting deserts, plus
material on the wildlife and plants.
An excellent hands-on narrative with
good pictures.

Okavango – Jewel of the Kalahari
by Karen Ross
(BBC Books, 1987)
A detailed look at the Kalahari Desert,
its climate, wildlife and human
inhabitants.

Physical Geology
by Judson and Kauffman
(Prentice Hall, 1990)
Academic but accessible book on
geological processes, with a good
chapter on winds and deserts,
explaining desert formation and
processes in lucid language.

The Secret Life of Animals
by Michael Bright
(Readers Digest, 1997)
Good on animal adaptations to desert
conditions, including 'air conditioned'
communities such as termites and
prairie dogs.

Wildlife of the Deserts
by Frederic H. Wagner
(Harry H, Abrams Inc. 1984)
Despite its age, this is a very
comprehensive guide to the
animals and plants of the desert, and
desert processes.

MAGAZINES

The Ecologist
Excellent articles on all aspects of conserving the planet, including frequent articles on deserts and desertification.

BBC Wildlife
Beautifully produced wildlife magazine for all ages, with a large variety of stimulating articles and regular columns, often dealing with desert-related subjects.

National Geographic
In-depth profiles of animals, regions and peoples, usually with stunning photos. Many articles on desert subjects listed in its enormous back catalogue index.

ORGANIZATIONS

WWF-UK
Panda House,
Weyside Park,
Godalming,
Surrey GU7 1XR
Tel: 01483 426444

Friends of the Earth
26-28 Underwood Street,
London N1 7JQ
Tel: 020 7490 1555

Greenpeace
Canonbury Villas,
London, N1 2PN
Tel: 020 7865 8100
Email: info@uk.greenpeace.org

Living Earth
4 Great James Street,
London WC1N 3DB
Tel: 020 7440 9750
Email: info@livingearth.org.uk

Survival International
6 Charterhouse Buildings,
London EC1M 7ET
Tel: 020 7687 8700
Email: info@survival-international.org

WEBSITES

www.theecologist.org
The website of *The Ecologist* magazine, which has an archive of all articles over the last two years.

www.unccd.int
The website of The United Nations Convention to Combat Desertification (UNCCD), with a very good series of fact sheets on the causes and effects of desertification, and links to a large amount of related material.

www.allafrica.com
The website of the Pan African News Agency, with links giving up-to-date stories on environment, country by country, in all regions of Africa.

www.eden-foundation.org
The website of the Eden Foundation, which gives specific and detailed information on the work it is doing to reverse desertification in Niger. Includes an excellent analysis of the problems of the Sahel region.

www.worldwildlife.org
The website of the World Wildlife Fund, with innumerable links to all aspects of conservation, and large amounts of information on species, environments, and specific campaigns.

INDEX